WORDS and MUSE Inks

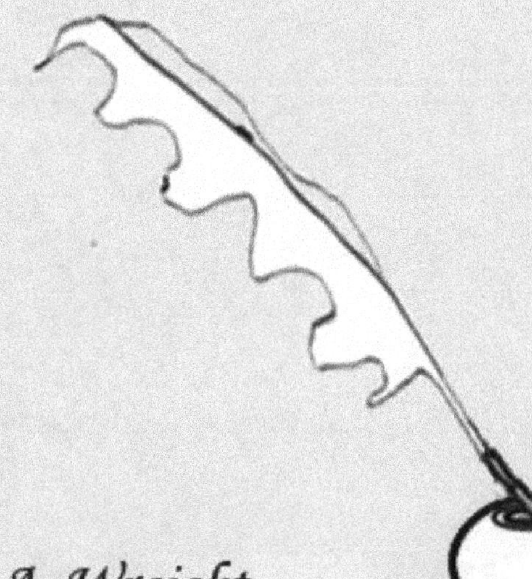

Text: Lois A. Wraight
Illustration: Evelyn Voigt

For Lois
with love
and admiration

HANGING AROUND the HOUSE:

Suspended in mid-lair

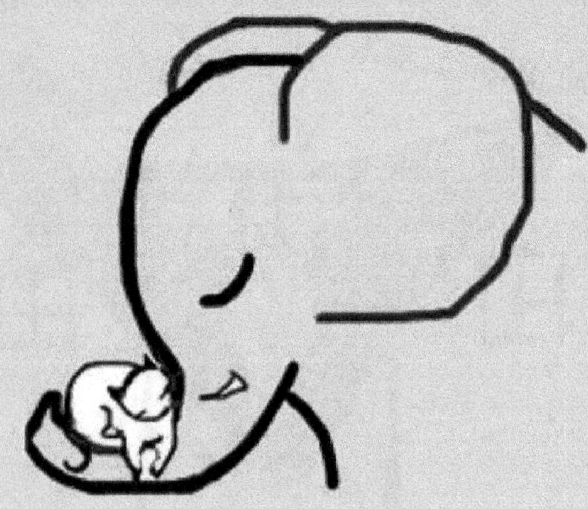

comfort
Zzzzzzzzzone

"Tonight. Tonight. Won't be like any night."

Two knights. Two knights.

Now that **would** *be a night...*

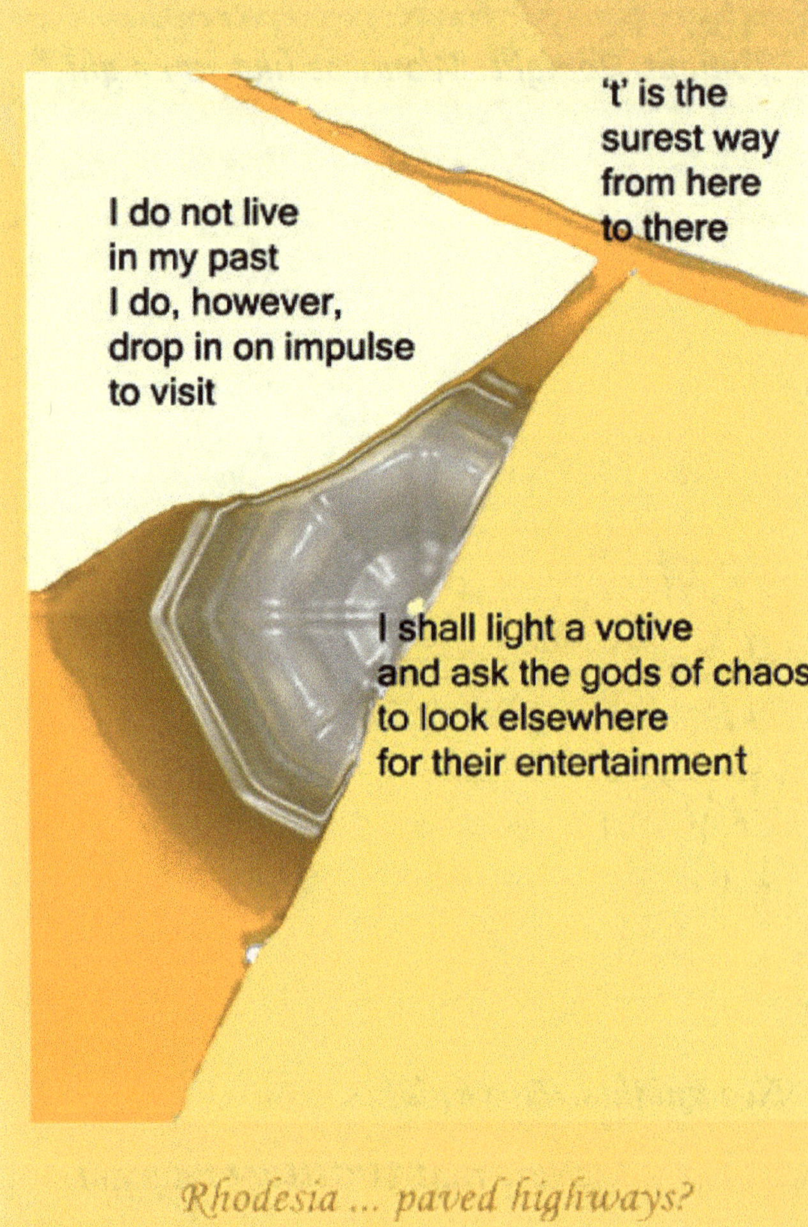
I do not live
in my past
I do, however,
drop in on impulse
to visit
'**t**' is the
surest way
from here
to there
I shall light a votive
and ask the gods of chaos
to look elsewhere
for their entertainment
Rhodesia ... paved highways?

AUTO-NEUROTICISM:
perceive me
if you see me at all
as staring back

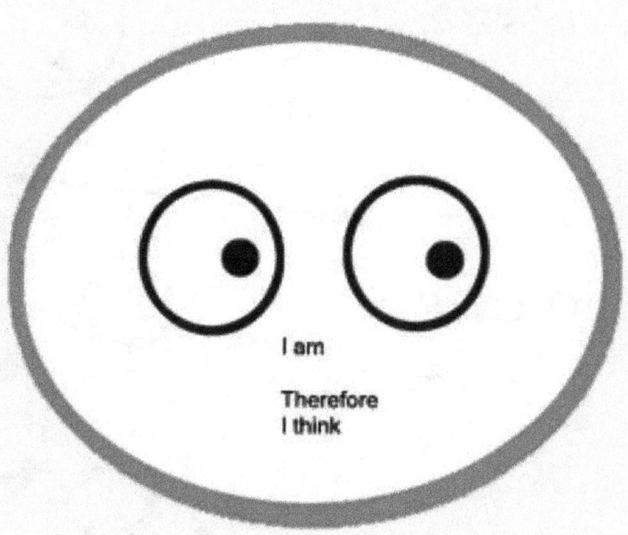

BREATHING: to air is human

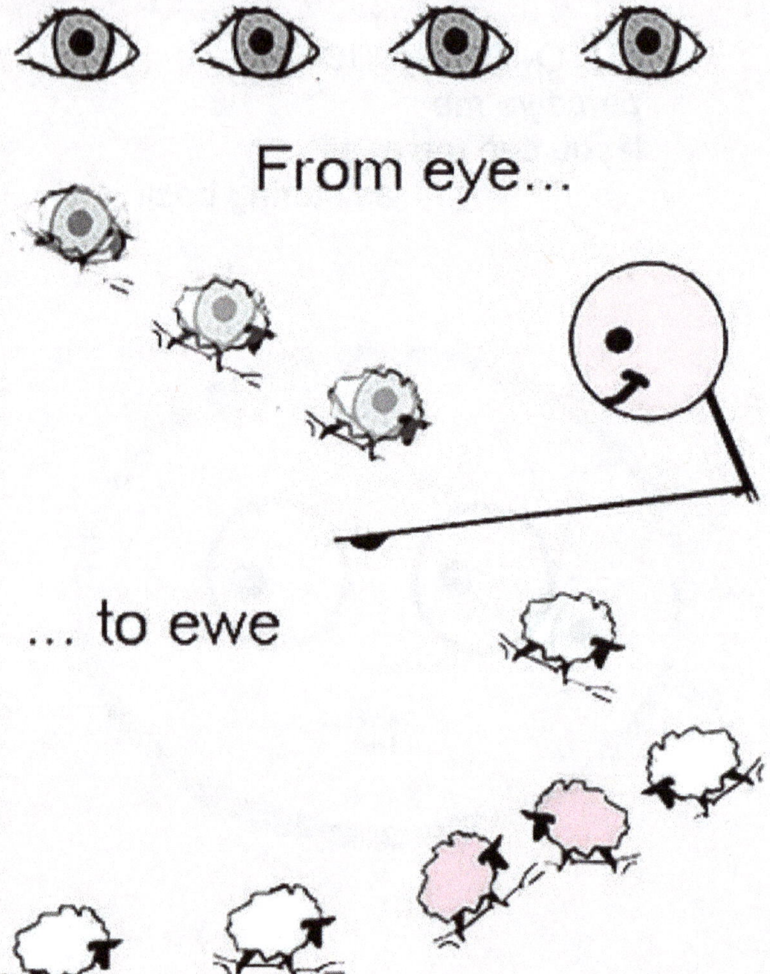
From eye...
... to ewe

surrealistic quadruped
with hump =

Salvador Dali llama

Surreal balks

I eat only cornflakes
I am a cereal monogamist

Using your head while pedalling: Tetracycline

rapid id movement; motor psyche

schizophrenia; bi psyche

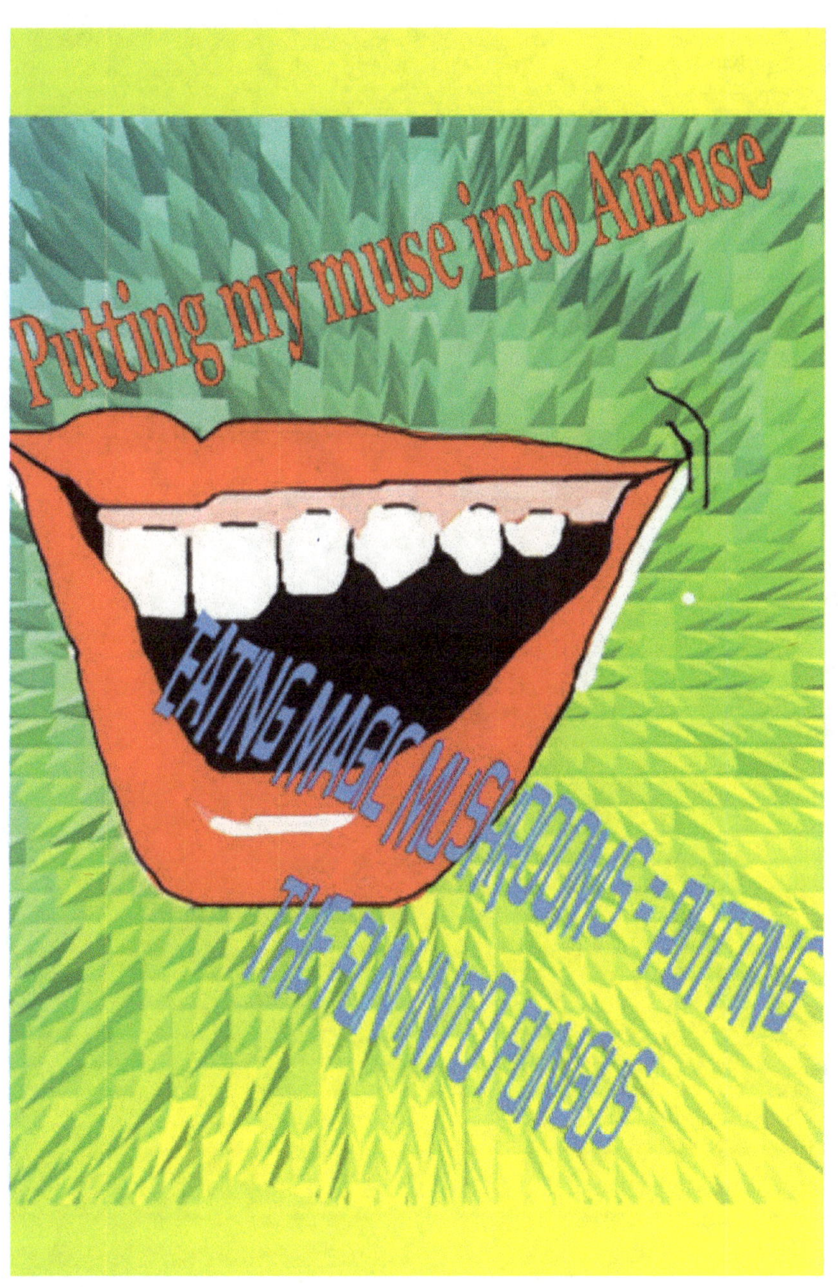
Putting my muse into Amuse
EATING MAGIC MUSHROOMS = PUTTING THE FUN INTO FUNGUS

DANCING TO SCHUBERT
follow the

L
I
E
D
E
R

R.S.V.P.
Re: *Umbilichorus,*
ms. Lois regrets
she will be unable
to add dis cord
to dat chord

<

Soprano to Schubert: Take me to your Lieder

intellectual snobbery =
haute culture

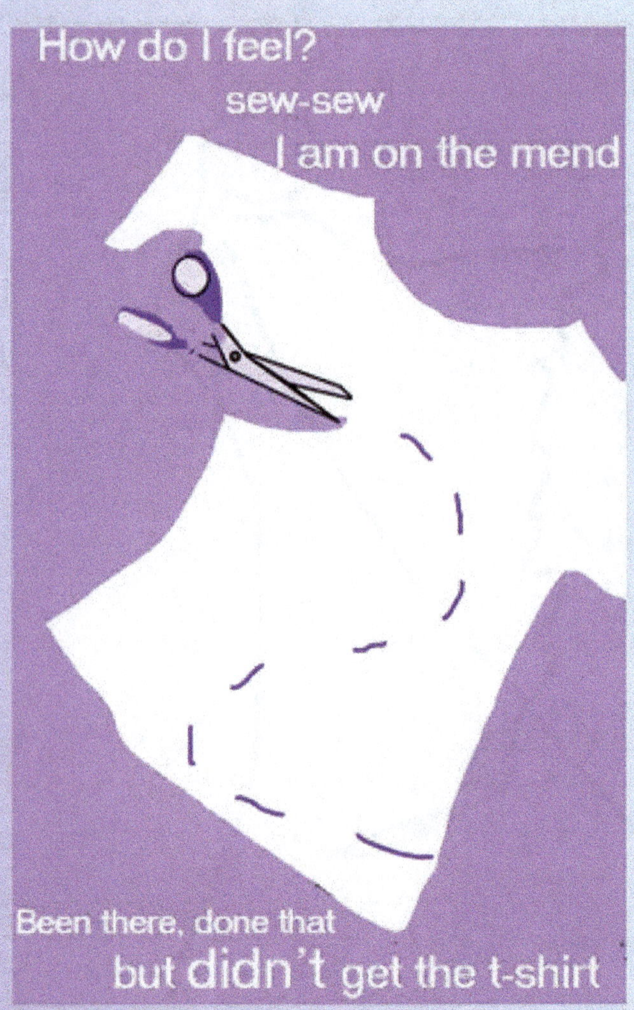
How do I feel?
sew-sew
I am on the mend
Been there, done that
but didn't get the t-shirt

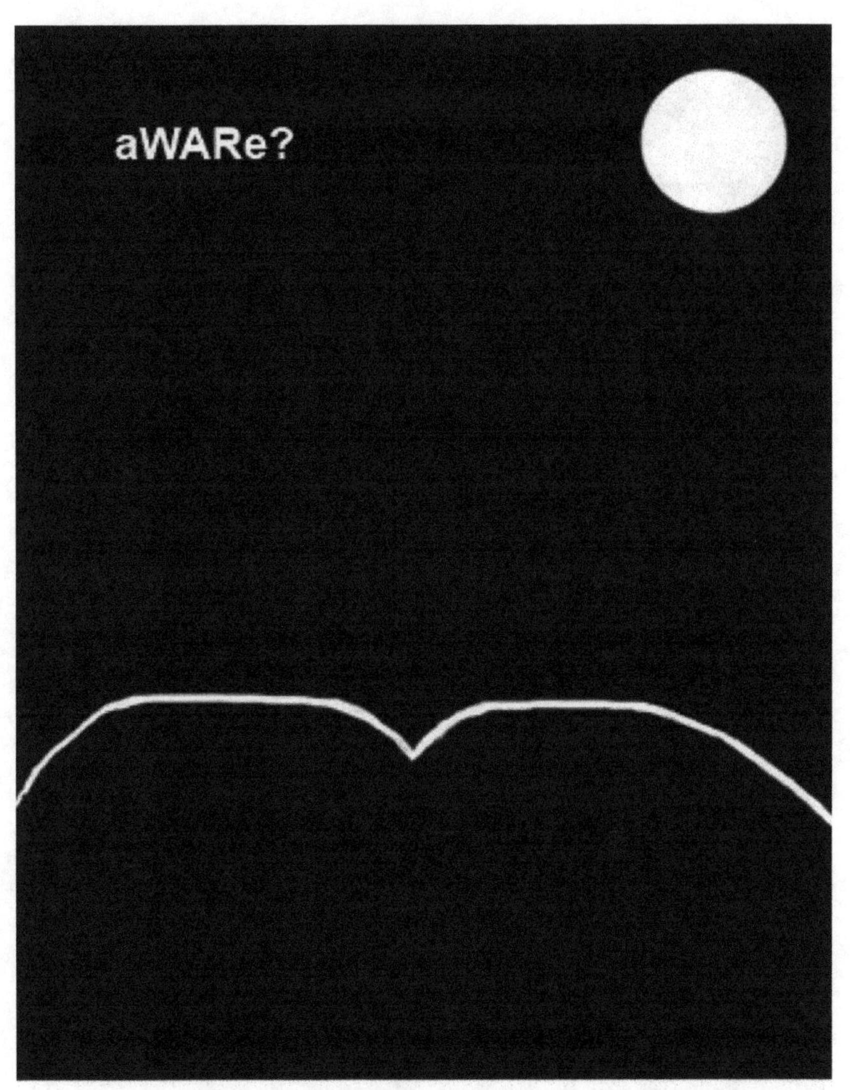

I would like to moon Bush
Or at least shake my pacifist

TENSE ELEVENTH HOUR

DEMOLITION CREWS;

EDIFICE WRECKS

PETS: THE PAWS THAT REFRESH

IF I HAD A DOG, I WOULD CALL HER 'TRUTH'
TRUTH ALWAYS COMES WHEN IT IS CALLED

DEFINITION OF A FRENCH POODLE

FAUX PAS

Making love
in the woods
is a
Black Fly
affair
First letter in the Canadian
alphabet: EH?

Other people's orgasms are anti-climactic

BUSH:
BETWEEN IRAQ
AND A HARD PLACE

hunger

the ultimate
eating
disorder

Never underestimate the power of Pacifism;

(no animals were harmed in the turning of this cheek).

Pacifism: march of the wouldn't soldiers

Kalahari Krishna
looking for truth
in a grain of Sand

Even Buddhist monks catch cold every Tao and Zen

What do you call a social worker
in a homeless shelter?
A succour for punishment

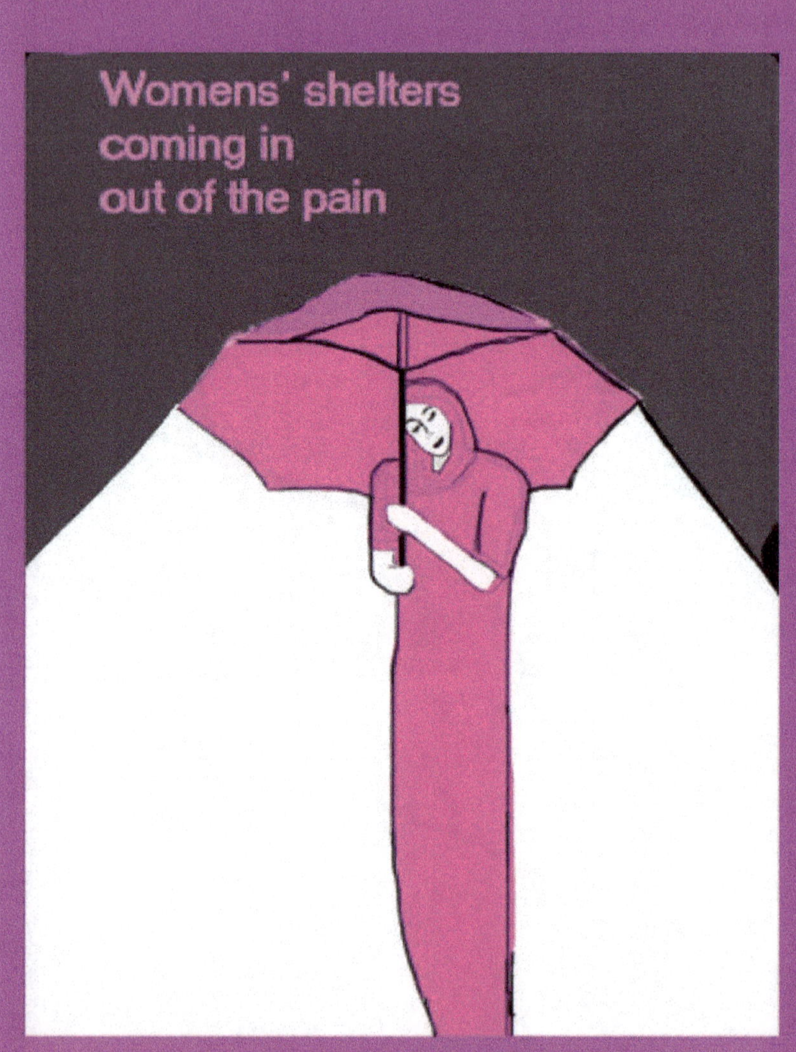
Womens' shelters
coming in
out of the pain
Pregnant teenager: didn't no

CONSERVATIONISTS

they're

their

deer.

Pray Now, Fly Later?

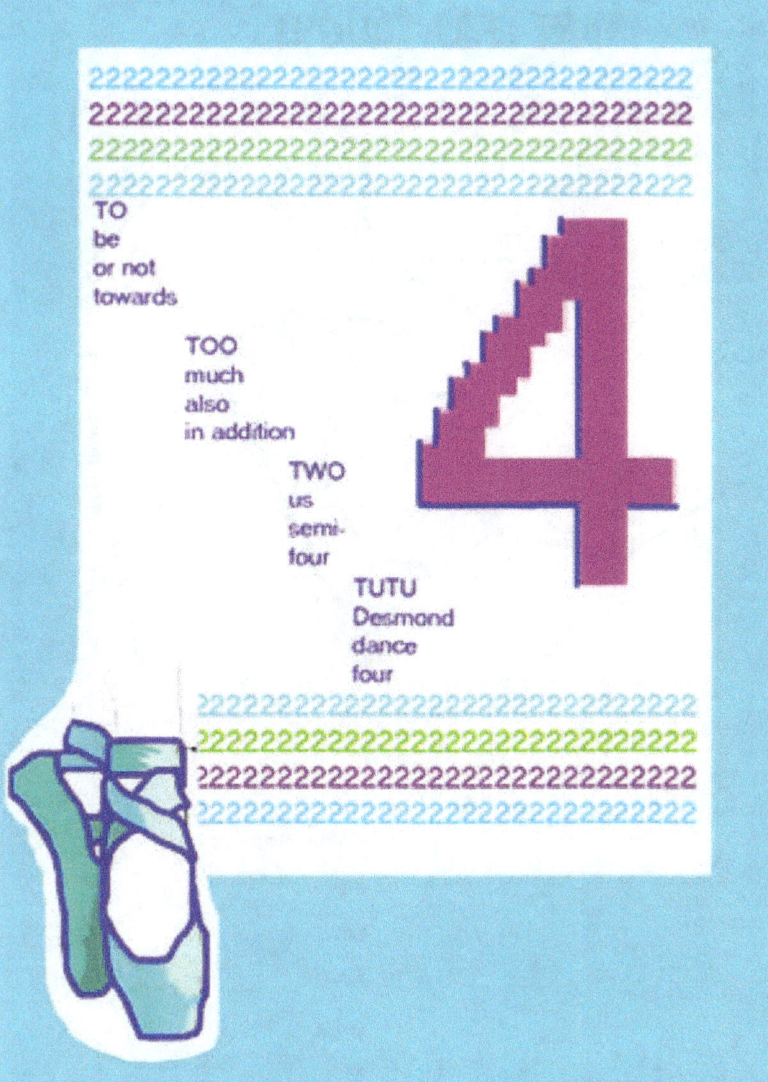
2222222222222222222222222222222222222
2222222222222222222222222222222222222
2222222222222222222222222222222222222
2222222222222222222222222222222222222
TO
be
or not
towards
TOO
much
also
in addition
TWO
us
semi-
four
TUTU
Desmond
dance
four
2222222222222222222222222222222
2222222222222222222222222222222
2222222222222222222222222222222
2222222222222222222222222222222

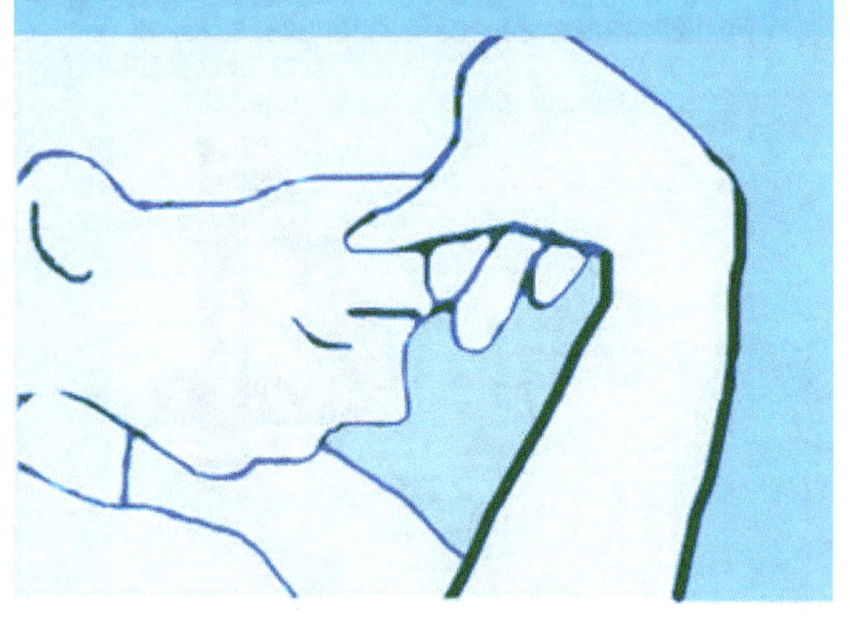

Baby Shower

itty

bitty

fes

tiv

ity

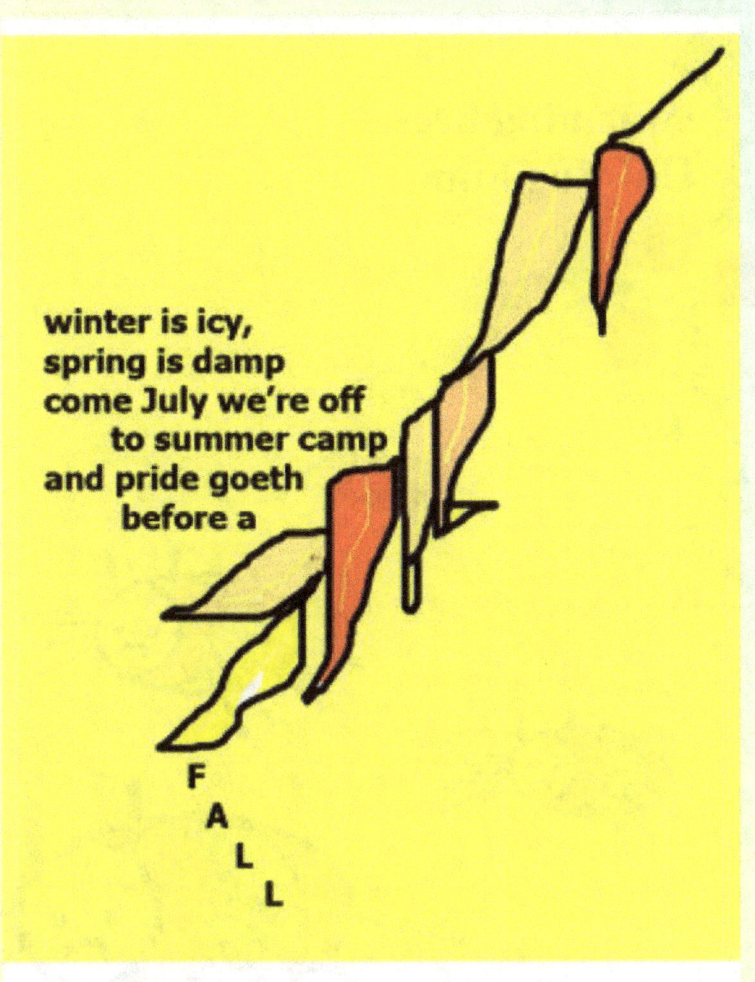

Deck the halls with boughs of colour
Fall lala lala, Fall la, la, la

swarming bees:
Ha! Bug hum

The thing
about spring is
it's so burgeoning
fecund
every second
fat, sloppy drops
fall from eaves
globules
that used to be winter

FLOWERS: things
that go bloom
in the light

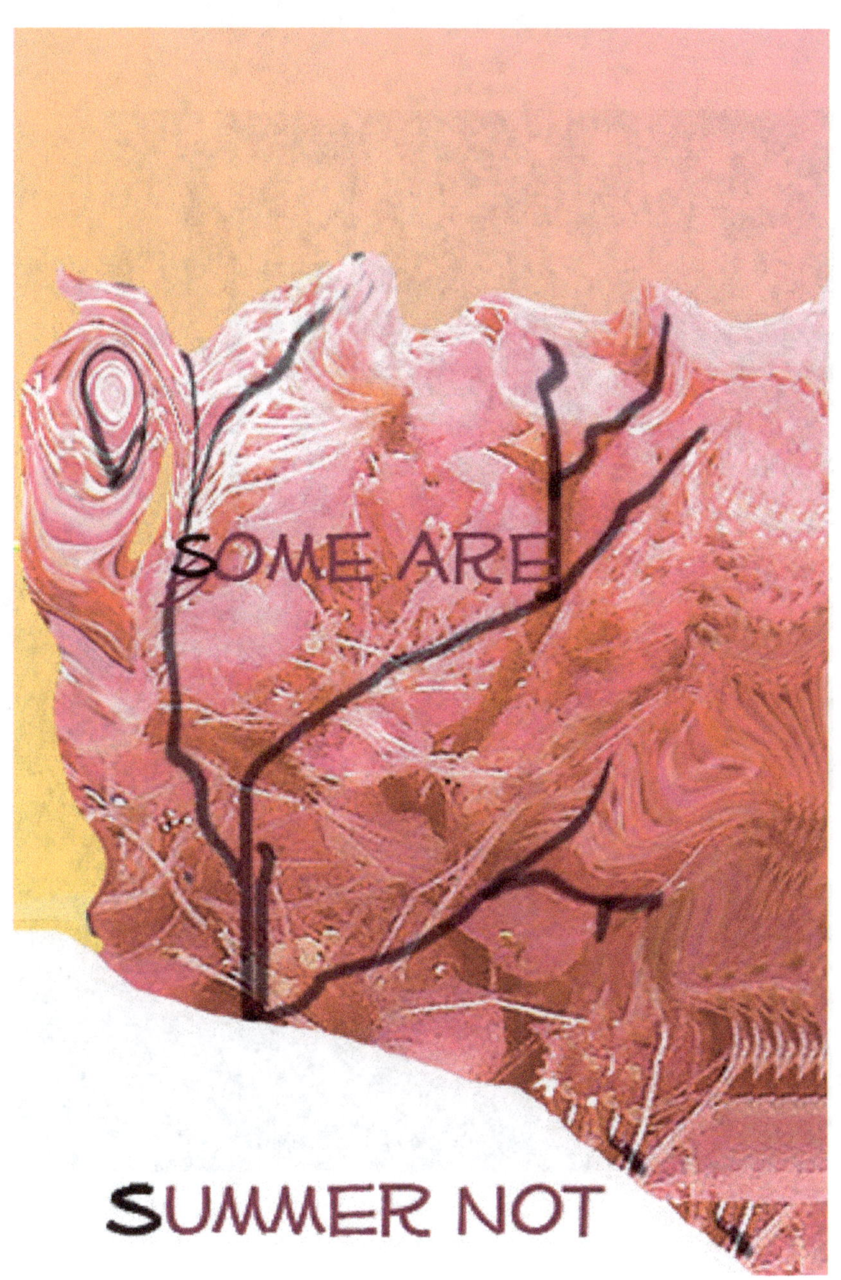
SOME ARE
SUMMER NOT

frozen leaves
life on ice

'A'
Christmas
is putting the advent
into adventure
Evelyn
puts the adventure
into advent

B'
bells call the faithful
the annual pilgrimage
of christmas Christians
to mass en masse
'C'
carry on
carolling
carillon

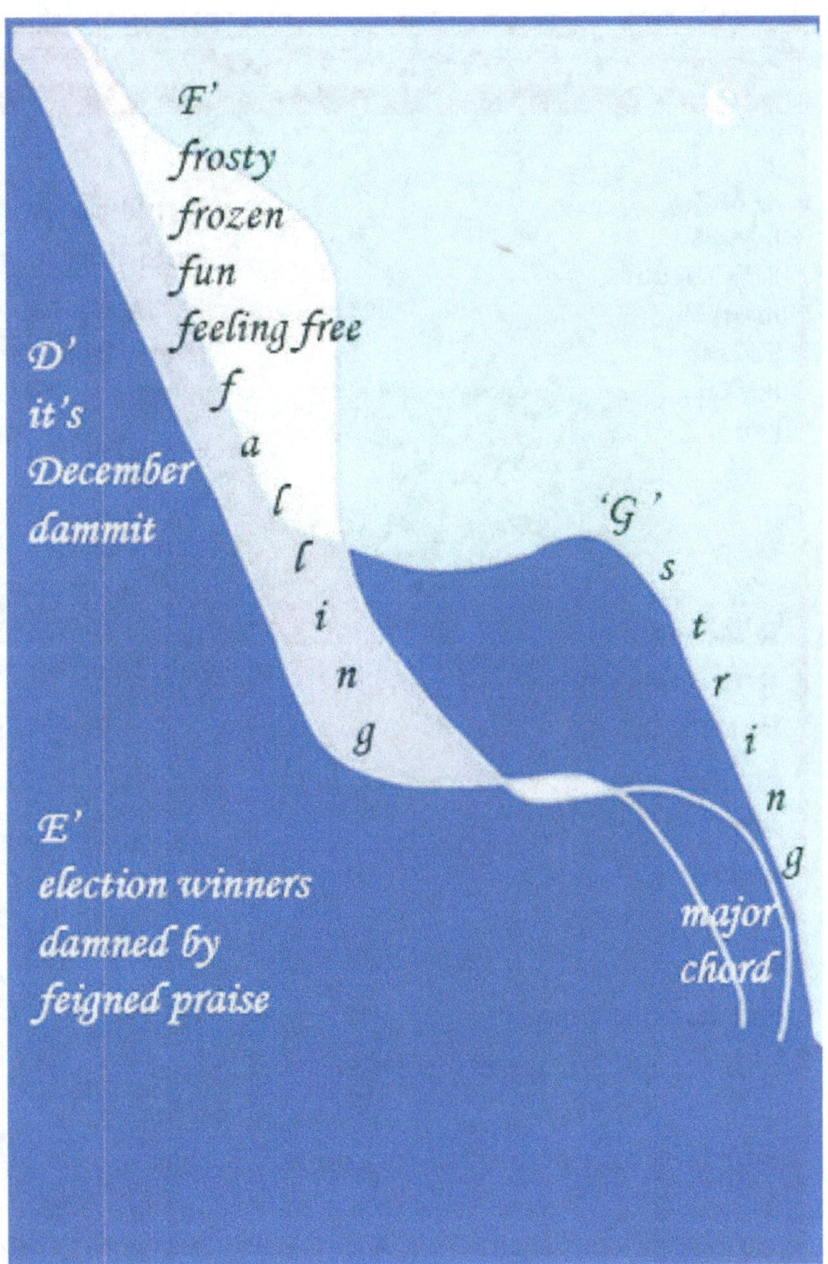
F'
frosty
frozen
fun
feeling free
f
a
l
l
i
n
g
D'
it's
December
dammit
'G'
s
t
r
i
n
g
E'
election winners
damned by
feigned praise
major
chord

H'
Ho Ho Hugs
Hallelujah
Happy Christmas
Hannukkah
Holocaust
Holy Cow
How?
I'
idiot ideologies
frozen thought
creating icy cull
corpses from the
killer corps of
idiocentricity's
icy kills
bloody icicles
J'
joy
to the world'
there's acid rains
let earth
her pain
survive
let every hurt
let every hearth
let every heart
and heaven and nature
sing?

'K'
kriick kraaack
the season's back
Kris Kringle
kisses and kindness
'peace on earth, goodwill to all'

would that we could distill it
dispense and consume at will it

'M'
Music that's maudlin and
merry
mistletoe and holly berries
magic and mysticism
for the alleged
son of Mary

'N'
name it and tame it
label and defame
yet, after, what
is in a name?

with cognomen else
I would still be myself

'L'
Little cat is lolling about
carelessly kittenish
unlady-like, uncaring
existentially loose
lost in her cats-only
consciousness
of self gratifiCATion
a Bast from the past

'O'
Oh Holy Night
that would be bliss
oh wholly night
that would be dark
oh holey night?
those would be stars
'P'
how many Jesuits
can you fit on the
head of a pin
who cares about this
or original sin?
why target pleasure
to identify transgressions
when war's the cardinal sin
demanding suppression?
'Q'
questions arise
doubting what Jesus did
asking why he died
what is the pro and quid
if it is a
question of faith
there is
no answer

‘R’

puRRing,

PUrrING

'S'

Mary christ-mess
saints and sinners
neither tops
my list of winners
siblings have sibilance
are very grand
I just hide my head
in an ampersand

•
t
his
tree is
exactly
the very tree
I wanted for me
My very first time,
t
his
exactly perfect wonderful
Christmas tree is fine and mine.
It lights from within, a glimmering, shining
string of glittering globes of pure golden delight
•
Let there be light. Let there be Light. LET THERE
BE LIGHT. Let there be light. Let there be light. LET THERE BE
LIGHT. Let there be light. Let there be Light. LET THERE BE
LIGHT
LIGHT
LIGHT
tTtTtTtTtTtTtTtTtTtTtTtTtTtTtTtTtTtTtTtTtTtTtTtTtTtTtTtTtTtTtTtTtT

‘U’
I do not think
it unreasonable
to be feeling
quite unseasonable
I’m much more prone
to ululating
than celebrating

‘V’
Did the vassals
from the castle
pillage the village
or was it holiday shoppers?

“It came upon a midnight clear”
Vixen was the only ‘v’ reindeer.

‘W’
if wishes
were Porshes
I’d still
rather walk

Inebriated farmer; Buccaholic.
Pastoral landscape without cows
or sheep; Scene but not herd.

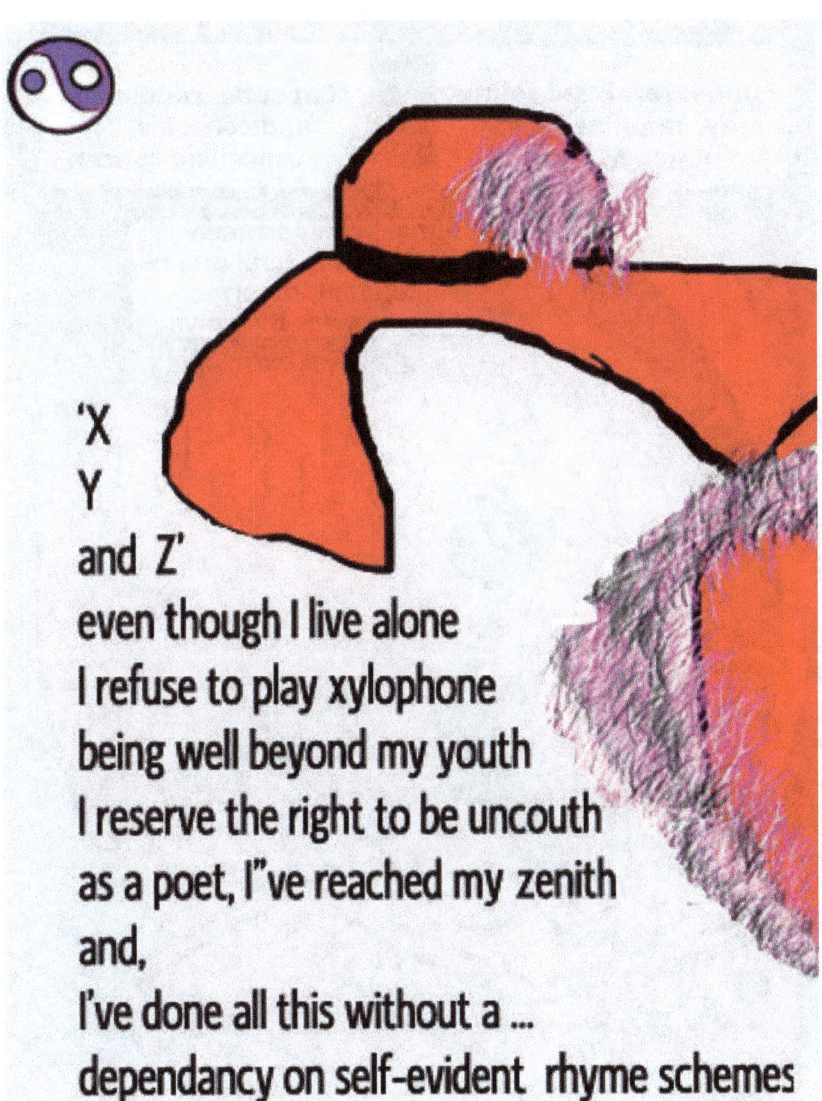

'X
Y
and Z'
even though I live alone
I refuse to play xylophone
being well beyond my youth
I reserve the right to be uncouth
as a poet, I"ve reached my zenith
and,
I've done all this without a ...
... dependancy on self-evident rhyme schemes

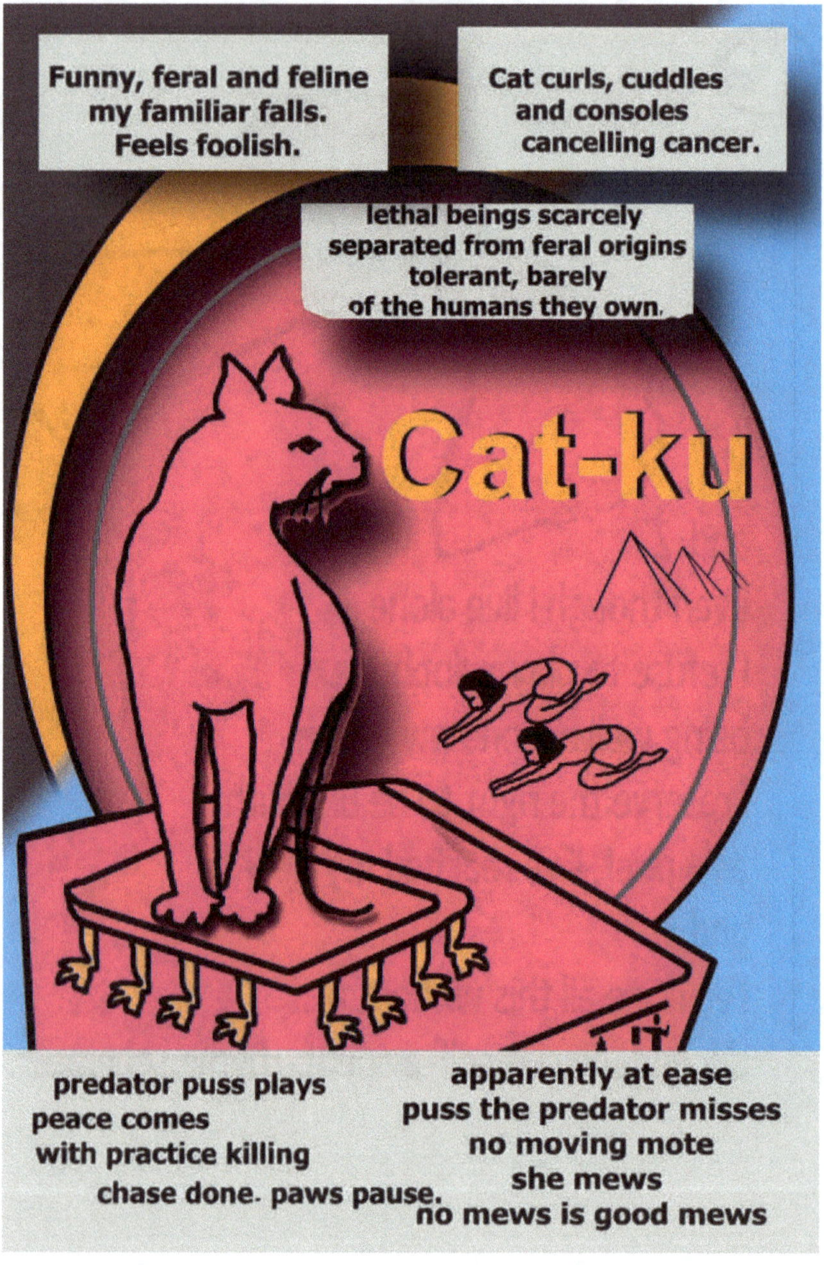

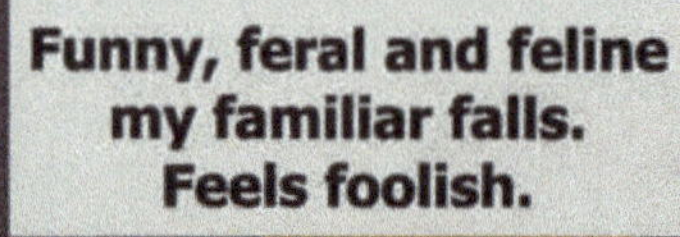

Funny, feral and feline
my familiar falls.
Feels foolish.
Cat curls, cuddles
and consoles
cancelling cancer.
lethal beings scarcely
separated from feral origins
tolerant, barely
of the humans they own.
Cat-ku
predator puss plays
peace comes
with practice killing
chase done. paws pause.
apparently at ease
puss the predator misses
no moving mote
she mews
no mews is good mews

Breathing -- to air is human

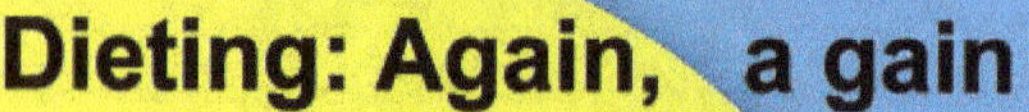

LEAVING AN EXHAUSTING APRIL BOYFRIEND

is letting the Aries out of her tired:

Naked goalie: Sports buff

School girls admiring sailors; Naval gazing.

Tombstone Humour
Last rites
for Wraight
who wrote
hence the term 'Blockhead'?

Audience at a performance of "Carmen": Bizet bodies.

Sarah Vaughn and Ella Fitzgerald did not sing so much as they caressed notes and blew kisses.

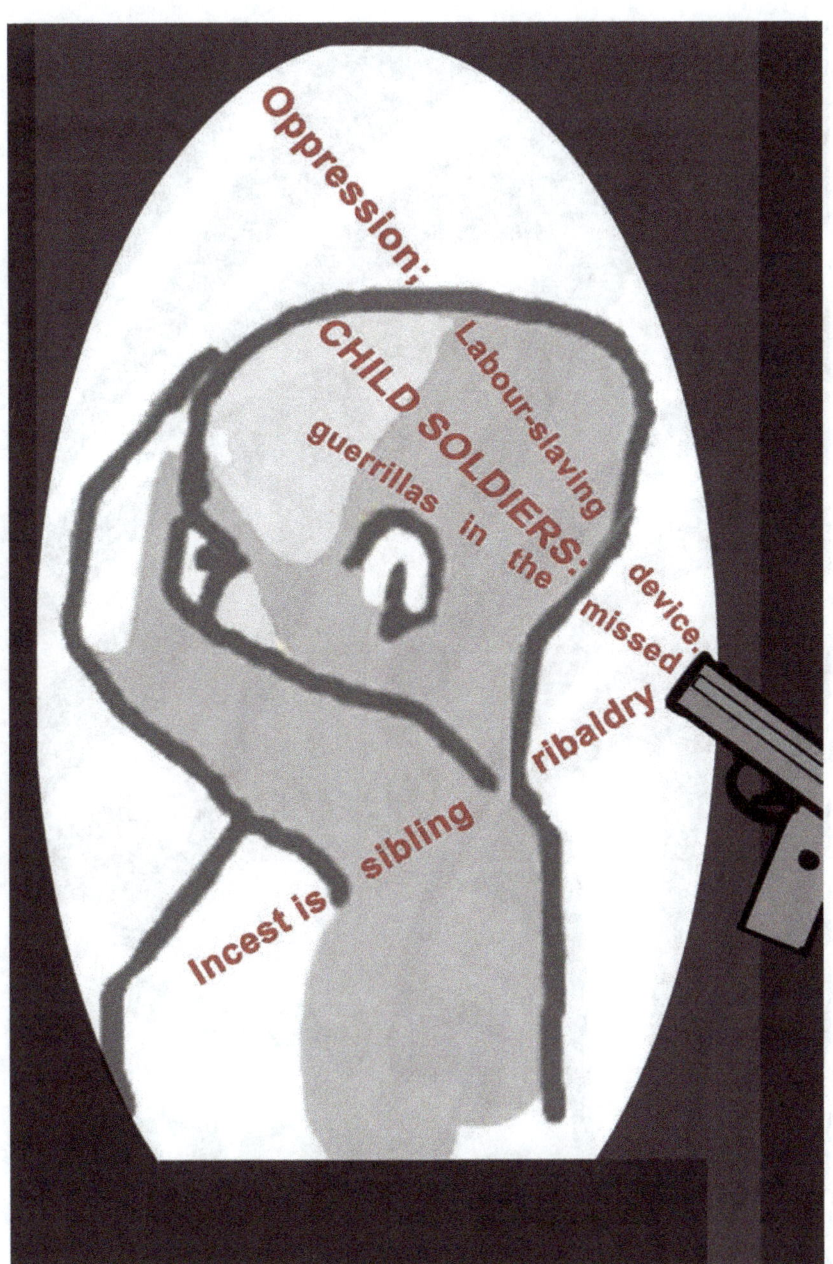
Oppression;
Labour-slaving
CHILD SOLDIERS:
guerrillas in the
device.
missed
ribaldry
sibling
Incest is

Fear

is just

the

qualm

before the

storm

60 seconds for every minute;
If there is a middle of things - I'm in it !
There was that moment and then - there wasn't.
Putting things off until tomorrow is demains - tia.

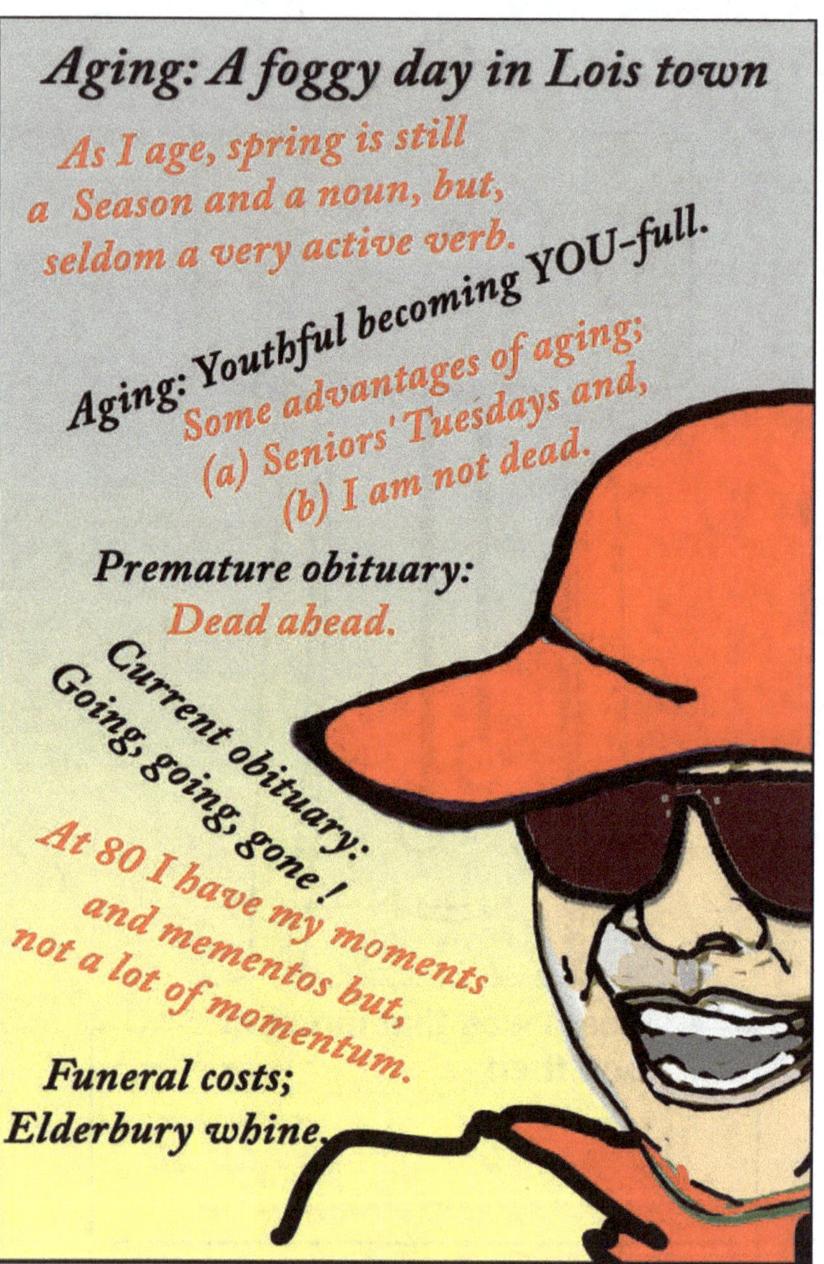
Aging: A foggy day in Lois town
As I age, spring is still
a Season and a noun, but,
seldom a very active verb.
Aging: Youthful becoming YOU-full.
Some advantages of aging;
(a) Seniors' Tuesdays and,
(b) I am not dead.
Premature obituary:
Dead ahead.
Current obituary:
Going, going, gone!
At 80 I have my moments
and mementos but,
not a lot of momentum.
Funeral costs;
Elderbury whine.

True incarceration is being locked-up in one's own brain cells.

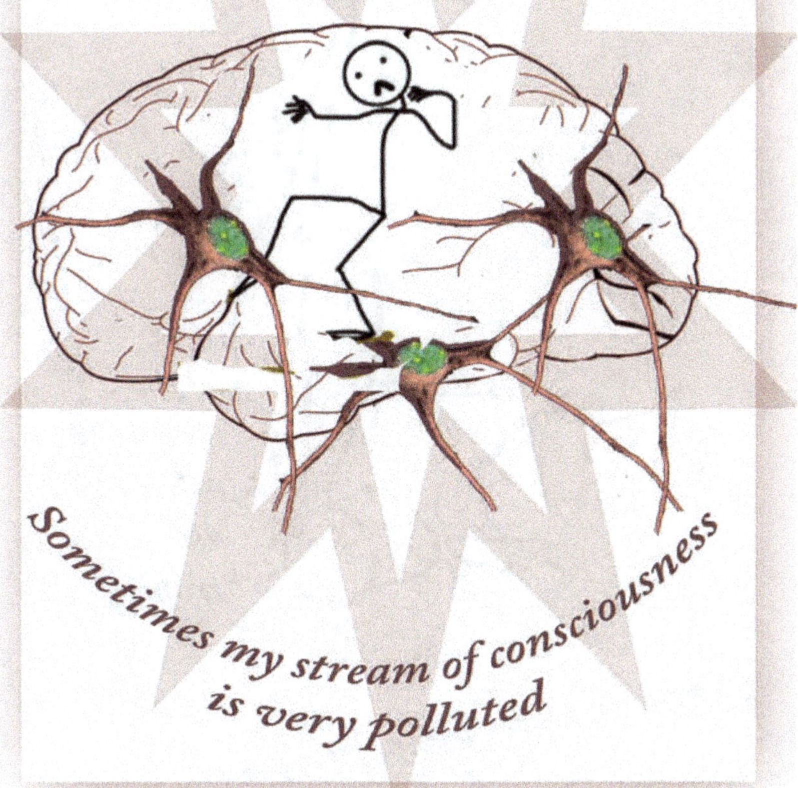

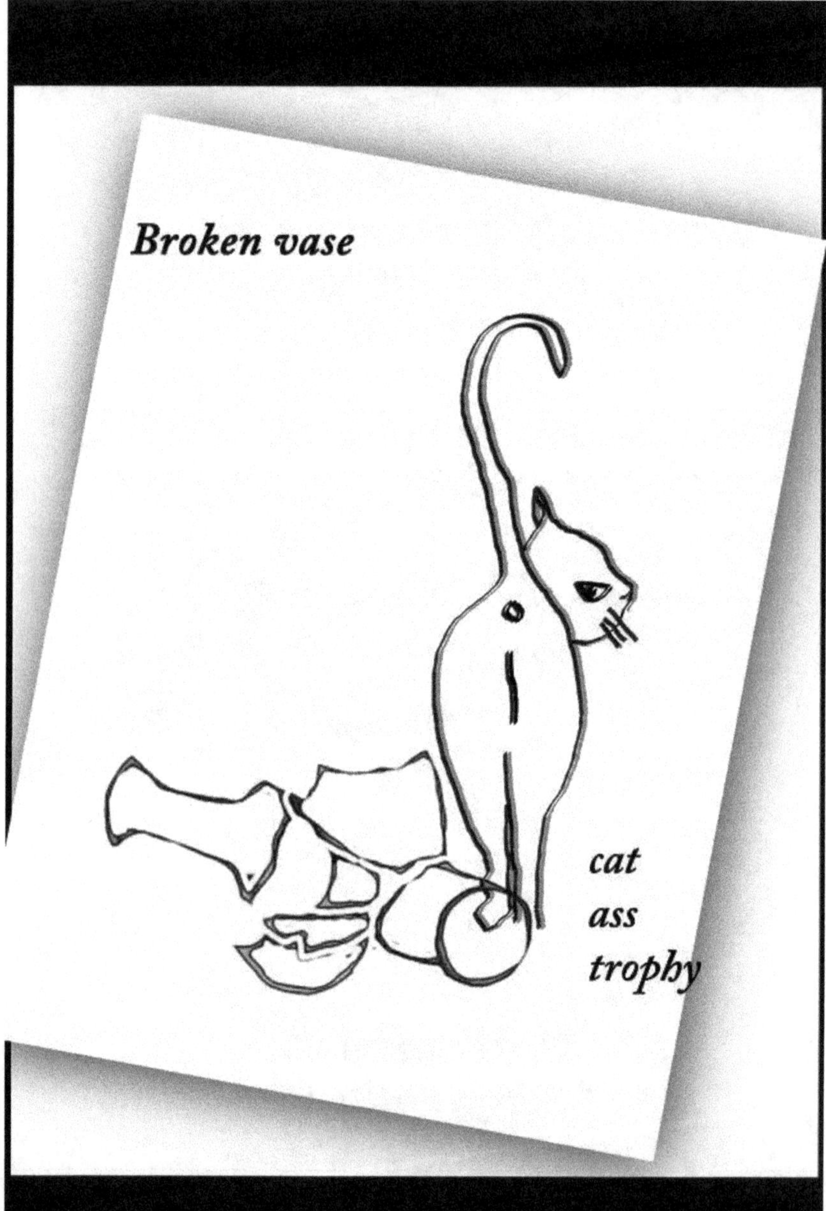
Broken vase
cat
ass
trophy

On being Canadian:
Chill slightly before serving.
Goose on a looney coin;
Canuck duck buck.
A Grizzly to the left
is a 'bear' sinister.
Wonder In Alice-Land; Hurrah for
Alice Monroe, Canadian Nobel-ity

Equine philosophers
always
put

Descarte
before
the horse..

Life: I know I have some of the answers, but, I seem to have forgotten the questions."

Maybe the concept of Peace is eluding us because it is difficult to conceive with a tilted Universe?

I bit into hard candy and cracked a crown; Tooth and consequences.

Came to town and didn't visit; flu' and no see ya

Political speechifying is talk sick.

Elected Officials:
Damned by feigned praise.

About wearing red on Fridays;
Frankly, dammit, I don't give a scarlet.

Why is it that every time
Stephen Harper opens his mouth, I
am reminded that Canada is the world's
largest producer and exporter of fertilizer?

Sara Pailin: bunny rabid

America's national
bird; The Bald Ego.

Let us keep the 'i' and 'h' away from trump.

Oaf of Allegiance, it is. " Never
underestimate the power of misogyny."

My cat thinks dog lovers

are purrverts.

"Uncarpeted steps cause blank stairs ."

Ideally, we'd live somewhere between Utopia and Dystopia. I, however, inevitably end up in Myopia.

We call trees whose
leaves fall in Autumn,
"DECIDuous";
Really ! Do you think they
DECIDed to go naked
all winter ?
leaves dying in beauty
crisp underfoot
play paths for children

Lois:
stark skeletal bones
of trees struck naked
presage winter
Evelyn:
released by winter
filigreed trees
caress eternity

Environmentalists have to green and bear it

Only 70 more shopping days 'til Christ Mass !

Christmas Potluck - Yule fuel ?

And to all you 'Snowbirds'

avoiding this seasonal phenomena

see me sticking out my tongue,

green with envy.

Christmas conflict: Presence vs. presents ?

Biographies:

Lois A. Wraight writes
and will
until the last
rites for Wraight

Evelyn voigt
global citizen
penning
for peace

Production editing:
Magdalene Carson, New Leaf Publication Design

www.ingramcontent.com/pod-product-compliance
Lightning Source LLC
LaVergne TN
LVHW052010160826
845678LV00005B/1706

* 9 7 8 1 7 7 7 3 6 7 7 7 0 *